KILLERS

BIRDS

PHILIP STEELE

Julian Messner

Copyright © 1991 by Julian Messner

First published by Heinemann Children's Reference,
a division of Heinemann Educational Books Ltd
Original Copyright © 1991 Heinemann Educational Books Ltd

Published by Julian Messner, a division of
Silver Burdett Press, Inc., Simon & Schuster, Inc.
Prentice Hall Bldg., Englewood Cliffs, NJ 07632

JULIAN MESSNER and colophon are trademarks of
Simon & Schuster, Inc.
U.S. project editor: Nancy Furstinger

Printed in Hong Kong

Lib. ed. 10 9 8 7 6 5 4 3 2 1
Paper ed. 10 9 8 7 6 5 4 3 2 1

Library of Congress Cataloging-in-Publication Data
Steele, Philip.
  Killers: birds/by Philip Steele.
   p. cm.
  Summary: Focuses on the feeding habits of several birds of prey
including the golden eagle, the gyrfalcon, and the kingfisher.
  1. Birds of prey – Juvenile literature. [1. Birds of prey.].
  I. Title.   90-32090
  QL696.F3S698 1991   CIP
  598–dc20   AC

   ISBN 0-671-72243-3 ISBN 0-671-72244-1 (pbk).

Photographic Acknowledgments
The author and publishers wish to acknowledge, with thanks, the following photographic sources:
a above *b* below *l* left *r* right
Cover photograph courtesy of Ardea/J Swedberg
Ardea 9*b* (C Haagner), 10 (R Smith), 15*b* (A Warren), 23*a* (W Mellor), 27*a* (J Bottomley), 28 (D Avon), 29 (P Steyn), 30*l* (J-P Ferrero), 31;
David Hosking 7*bl*; 8*r*; Eric Hosking 11*b*; 21*b*, 22*a*; Frank Lane 6 (D Holland), 8*l* (L Robinson), 9*a* (W Wisniewski), 20 (L Barren), 21*a* (S
Jonasson), 22*b* (A Hamblin), 25*r* (R Tidman), 30*r* (A Hamblin); NHPA 7*a* (A Bannister), 13*a* (M Danegger), 13*b* (H van Ingen), 15*a* (E
Murtomaki), 18 (S Dalton), 19 (A Bannister), 23*b* (P Johnson), 24 (P Scott), 25*a* and *l* (E James), 26 (M Leach), 27*b* (S Dalton); Survival
Anglia 7*b* (D & M Plage), 11*a* (J Foott).
The publishers have made every effort to trace the copyright holders, but if they have inadvertently overlooked any, they will be pleased
to make the necessary arrangement at the first opportunity.

CONTENTS

BIRDS THAT KILL	6
The risk of attack	7
A bird's weapons	7
GROUND ATTACK	8
The biggest bird alive	8
Cassowaries	9
The snake-killer	9
KILLER KINGS	10
The golden eagle	10
The bald eagle	11
The monkey-killer	11
AERIAL AMBUSH	12
Buzz bombs	13
Low flier	13
DEATH FROM THE SKY	14
The speed star	14
The chaser	15
The crested caracara	15
ACCESSORIES TO MURDER	16
In at the kill	16
The high fliers	17
EYES IN THE NIGHT	18
Eating habits	18
Snowy owl	19
Barn owl	19
PIRATES OF THE HIGH SEAS	20
The bullies	20
The torpedoes	21
The man-o'-war birds	21
FISHER FOES	22
Stabbers of the swamps	22
The shoebill	23
The kingfishers	23
NEST-RAIDERS	24
Common jay	24
Pied currawong	24
Common cuckoo	25
CITY GANGSTERS	26
Birds as pests	27
Scare tactics	27
CROP-RAIDERS	28
The scourge of Africa	28
SAVING THE BIRDS	30
Birds at risk	31
Index	32

BIRDS THAT KILL

★ Did you know that birds are distant relatives of snakes and crocodiles? This is because the first birds that appeared on Earth about 150 million years ago developed from reptiles. Some of them had feathered bodies and toothy jaws.

T ODAY, birds have feathers but no teeth. Unlike reptiles, they are warm-blooded. Their bodies always stay at the same temperature. Most birds can fly.

Some birds eat seeds and fruits. Other eat carrion, or dead animals. Still others, called birds of prey or predators, kill live animals.

White-breasted sea eagle

THE RISK OF ATTACK

MOST birds are harmless. Some may attack humans in self-defense and injure them. However, they very rarely kill people. Some birds may cause the death of humans indirectly. They may destroy large areas of crops or spread diseases. Others may cause accidents. For example, if a bird is sucked into the engine of a jet, the plane may crash.

Flying birds cannot weigh too much, or they would not be able to take off. For the same reason, the loads they lift cannot be too heavy. Therefore, birds do not prey on live humans. The largest animals preyed upon by birds are young deer, antelopes, and seals.

Martial eagle

A BIRD'S WEAPONS

BIRDS are perfectly designed for the job of killing their prey. Over time many have developed amazing weapons for survival. Some have sharp claws, or talons, for gripping their victims. Some have powerful, hooked beaks for tearing at flesh. Some have very powerful limbs that can strike forcefully. They can use their wings as clubs when attacking, or as a shield to protect themselves.

Bald eagle beak

Fisheagle talons

GROUND ATTACK

OST birds of prey need to fly. They hunt from the air. Many of the smaller birds they feed on also fly. They need to escape quickly. However, not all birds fly. Some get around by other means. Penguins can swim up to 22 miles per hour. Ostriches can run 45 miles per hour. Birds that live on the ground are easy targets for hunters and wild animals. Many of them have become extinct. Some have learned to fight back.

THE BIGGEST BIRD ALIVE

HE flightless ostrich lives off seeds, plant shoots, worms, and lizards. It is hardly designed as a killer. However, it is the largest bird of all. It is 8 feet high and weighs almost 300 pounds. It also has very powerful legs and razor-sharp claws. Ostriches can inflict serious injury, and can even kill. Males are particularly dangerous during the mating season. They will charge almost anything that moves.

CASSOWARIES

THE cassowaries are flightless birds that live in the rain forests of New Guinea and northern Australia. Some are up to 6½ feet tall. They have a bony helmet on their head. This protects the bird's head when it charges through thick bushes. Cassowaries are shy. However, if one is cornered, it strikes out. The toes have claws and a spike. Cassowaries have been known to kill humans.

THE SNAKE-KILLER

THE secretary bird of Africa is able to fly. However, it spends most of the day on the ground, hunting rodents and snakes. If a snake strikes back, the bird protects itself with its wing. It kills the snake by striking it with its powerful foot. Secretary birds are 4 feet high. They can injure humans.

KILLER KINGS

E AGLES are huge, powerful predators with curved beaks and sharp claws. For centuries people thought of them as royal birds. In some parts of the world, chiefs wore eagle feathers, and royalty chose the eagle for their emblem.

A noble family

Eagles can be divided into four main groups.
★ The true eagles have legs that are covered by feathers all the way down to their toes.
★ The fish eagles have bare lower legs, or tarsi. Their feet have small ridges to grip slippery fish.
★ The snake-eating eagles also have bare tarsi, but they are covered by tough scales. This protects them against snake bites.
★ The harpy eagle and its relatives are very large eagles with thick, powerful legs.

THE GOLDEN EAGLE

T HE golden eagle once lived all over the northern half of the world. Today, this true eagle is rare in many countries. Farmers shot it because they believe eagles kill their sheep. Golden eagles may attack sick lambs, but they do not harm flocks. Their normal prey are rabbits, hares, birds, snakes, and rodents. They also eat carrion.

The golden eagle is now protected by law in many places. It lives in remote mountainous regions. It is 35 inches long, with a wingspan of almost 6 feet. This predator flies over vast areas and scans the ground for food.

THE BALD EAGLE

S LIGHTLY larger than the golden eagle, the American bald eagle is our national symbol. It is a fish eagle.

The bald eagle is on the endangered species list. Its populations suffered greatly after many bald eagles injested insecticides. This caused females to lay eggs with thin or no shells. Also, the waters where it hunted have been drained, and its nesting trees chopped down. Fortunately, many people are working to save it.

THE MONKEY-KILLER

T HE very rare monkey-eating eagle is found only in the Philippine Islands. This fierce relative of the harpy eagle lives in forests. Its nesting site is marked by piles of bones discarded after meals. It eats monkeys, squirrels, birds, and dogs. About 3 feet long, the monkey-eating eagle is one of the largest eagles.

AERIAL AMBUSH

THE goshawks and sparrow hawks live in many parts of the world. They have a fierce stare, and long yellow legs with black talons. The largest is the Northern goshawk, a forest dweller more than 23 inches long. The black-mantled goshawk of New Guinea is about 14 inches long.

Many goshawks are experts at ambush. They can remain still for a long time. Then they dart after large woodland birds at high speeds.

Sparrow hawks are fast fliers. They hunt small birds in hedges and trees.

Black-mantled goshawk

Northern goshawk

BUZZ BOMBS

BUZZARDS are large hawks. They may be up to 23 inches long, with a wingspan of 5 feet. The common buzzard lives in wooded valleys in mountainous areas. It perches, soars, and hovers, searching for rabbits, birds, snakes, and carrion.

The rough-legged buzzard is found on bare mountain sides and in the frozen Arctic. There it hunts small rodents called lemmings. In years when there are more lemmings, the buzzards lay more eggs.

Common buzzard

LOW FLIER

THERE are 17 species of harriers. The marsh harrier of North Africa, Europe, and Asia hunts water voles, frogs, and waterfowl. Its prey often hides in dense reed beds, so the harrier flies in low and slow.

Montagu's harrier is often found on dry wastelands or near pine woods. It feeds on small birds, snakes, and lizards.

Montagu's harrier

DEATH FROM THE SKY

FALCONS are smaller predators than hawks and eagles, but they are deadly. Their long, pointed wings are streamlined for speed.

Falconry

The sport of hunting small birds or animals with falcons is called falconry. It was very popular in Europe until the seventeenth century. It is still practiced today.

THE SPEED STAR

THE peregrine falcon is a beautiful, gray-backed falcon that grows up to 19 inches in length. It is found all over the world. Its favorite victims are pigeons. It attacks them in a headlong dive at speeds of 80 miles per hour or more. It is one of the fastest birds in the world.

THE CHASER

THE gyrfalcon is the largest falcon of all. It is about 20 inches long. It hunts the bare lands of the Arctic. To hunt, it runs after birds and grabs them from behind. Gyrfalcons are usually brownish-gray, but in Greenland they are white and blend in with the snow.

Gyrfalcon

THE CRESTED CARACARA

CARACARAS are falcons that hunt on the ground. They prefer to eat carrion, but they do kill wounded or sick animals, too. The crested caracara lives in South and Central America and the southern United States. It eats lizards, baby alligators, and turtles. It will also tackle larger prey. It often eats dead giant rodents called capybaras. Caracaras have long, powerful legs and are about 24 inches in length.

Crested caracara

ACCESSORIES TO MURDER

V ULTURES are large, ugly birds that feed on carrion. Since vultures rarely kill living prey, they do not have gripping claws and powerful beaks like other predators. Instead, they have bald necks, so that they can easily poke their head far into a carcass to find scraps of flesh. They have powerful wings, and soar high into the air. This allows them to spot a dying animal from far away.

Vultures may seem to be gruesome birds. However, they perform a useful job, as they clean up the countryside.

★ **Thirteen kinds of vultures are found in Europe, Asia, and Africa. These are the Old-World vultures and they are related to eagles. The seven kinds found in the Americas, or the New World, are in a group of their own.**

IN AT THE KILL

T HE Egyptian, eared, and griffon are Old-World vultures. The Egyptian vulture is more than 25 inches long, and scavenges around villages. The eared and griffon vultures are more than 3 feet in length. They will eat any carrion — even humans.

Eared vulture

Griffon vulture

Egyptian vulture

THE HIGH FLIERS

T HE condors of the Americas are mountain vultures. The Californian condor no longer exists in the wild. The Andean condor is the heaviest bird of prey. It weighs more than 24 pounds. It has a wingspan of over 9 feet and can soar more than 2½ miles high looking for carrion or even live prey.

Andean condor

Californian condor

EYES IN THE NIGHT

OWLS are among the most efficient birds of prey. They hunt mostly by night, and silently, except for an occasional hoot or shriek. Owls have large heads and huge eyes that face forward. They can swivel their heads, and their eyesight is excellent. They also have very sharp hearing. Like other predators, owls have curved beaks and sharp talons. Watch out when going near their roost. They can seriously injure human intruders.

EATING HABITS

THE diets of owls vary. Many species eat insects, rats, and mice. Some eat rabbits, hares, skunks, squirrels, small birds, and fish. They eat their prey whole. Bones, fur, and other parts that are hard to digest are squeezed into a pellet and coughed up.

The horned and eagle owls are the biggest of all. Each species is about 24 inches long. The spotted eagle owl lives in southern Africa. It hunts for its prey in rocky, open country, among scrub and bushes.

Spotted eagle owl

★ Owls are found in most parts of the world. There are 123 kinds of true owls, and 10 species of barn owls.

SNOWY OWL

T HE white feathers of the snowy owl help to conceal it against the Arctic snow. It has black talons and a black beak, and is about 26 inches long. It hunts by day, feeding on lemmings. When they grow scarce, the owls move farther south. Unlike most owls, snowy owls nest on the ground.

Snowy owl

BARN OWL

T HE barn owl is found almost everywhere. In some countries, however, it is becoming rare. That is because the forests, where it often lives, are being cut down. Also, the mice it eats are being poisoned by chemicals used on farms. The barn owl is about 13 inches long.

Barn owl

PIRATES OF THE HIGH SEAS

SEABIRDS eat mostly fish, but many, such as the gull, also eat nestlings and carrion. Many seabirds are very aggressive. They steal prey from other birds and even attack humans who come too near their nests. Fulmars and albatrosses may spit out a foul, sticky oil in self-defense.

THE BULLIES

SKUAS are cousins of the gulls. Their beaks have hooked tips and there are powerful claws on the end of their webbed toes. They are very aggressive. The great skua breeds around the bitterly cold coastlines of the Arctic and the Antarctic. It lives near penguin colonies, stealing eggs and killing young birds. It also kills puffins, kittiwakes, and lemmings. The great skua will attack birds as large as herons. It sometimes attacks seabirds in flight and steals the fish they have caught.

Great skua

THE TORPEDOES

MANY seabirds hunt fish by diving. Some dive from the surface. Others dive from the air. The gannet dives from a height of almost 100 feet. It hits the water at high speed. Its 35-inch-long body and its skull are designed to withstand the huge shock of impact. The bird spears fish with its beak, and swallows them whole before it resurfaces.

THE MAN-O'-WAR BIRDS

YEARS ago, warships were known as "men-o'-war." Man-o'-war birds were named this because they, too, were aggressive fighters. Today they are known as frigate birds. About 3 feet long, they live in the warm coastal waters of the Pacific and Atlantic oceans. They kill turtles, fish, jellyfish, and nestling birds. They catch flying fish in midair. During the mating season, they rob each other of their catch. They seize the prey of other birds. During this season, the male has a bright-red throat. He puffs it out to attract females.

Great frigate bird

FISHER FOES

WATER birds have many weapons to kill their prey. Their beaks may be pointed for stabbing, or saw-edged for gripping slippery fish. Some beaks may be thin and curved, for probing in the mud. Many birds have long legs, for standing in water while fishing.

STABBERS OF THE SWAMPS

THE white stork stands about 3 feet tall. It is a wading bird with long red legs and a powerful, spearlike red beak. It hunts for small wetland creatures. The white stork breeds in Asia and in central Europe, often nesting on roofs. Each year, the European white storks migrate to Africa for the winter.

White stork

Great white heron

The great white heron is found around the Gulf of Mexico. It is another large wading bird. Like the stork, the heron has a long, deadly beak, and stiltlike legs for wading. It has a powerful, muscular neck that strikes quickly. The great white heron hunts for fish and crabs in coastal pools and salt marshes.

THE SHOEBILL

I N Africa, in the south of Sudan, the Nile River becomes lost in a vast swamp. This is the home of an odd-looking killer, the shoebill. Sometimes known as the whale-headed stork, this bird is more like a heron than a stork. It is about 5 feet tall, and has long legs and one of the strangest-looking beaks of any bird. It uses this beak to gulp down catfish and lungfish, as well as frogs, turtles, and crocodile hatchlings.

THE KINGFISHERS

N OT all freshwater birds are waders. The kingfishers are divers. Their dagger-shaped beak grips fish rather than stabs them. Kingfishers are found in many parts of the world. The giant kingfisher of Africa is the largest of its kind. It is 16 inches long. It may dive from an overhanging branch. It also may hover in the air before diving.

Giant kingfisher

NEST-RAIDERS

MANY birds kill their own species. They steal eggs and eat nestlings. The victims of such attacks have developed ways to hide. Many of the eggs are speckled. This makes them hard to see against the ground. Chicks may have speckled feathers or patterns that fool predators.

COMMON JAY

LIKE many members of the crow family, the 15-inch-long common jay is a terrible enemy of other woodland birds during the nesting season. From the United States to Asia, it seizes eggs and nestlings with its powerful beak. The jay also kills mice and insects to add to its usual diet of acorns, nuts, and berries.

PIED CURRAWONG

THIS 18-inch-long Australian mountain magpie will eat almost anything. It dines on carrion and insects, and raids orchards and gardens. It also eats eggs and nestlings.

COMMON CUCKOO

T HE common cuckoo of Europe and Asia is 13 inches long. It eats mostly insects and caterpillars. However, the cuckoo is a threat to other birds, because it lays its eggs in their nests. The cuckoo removes one egg from the nest. The foster parents do not notice the strange egg, and hatch it. The young cuckoo then throws out any other nestlings or eggs in the nest. The foster parents feed the young cuckoo, often until it is bigger than they are.

1 A cuckoo's egg was laid in a dunnock's nest.

2 This cuckoo chick has killed the young pipits.

3 An adult reed warbler feeds a young cuckoo.

CITY GANGSTERS

MANY birds have adapted to life in cities. The buildings provide warmth, and there is plenty of food to scavenge. Small birds such as pigeons and sparrows live there. Birds of prey have moved in to hunt them and the small rodents that live in lots and parks. The common kestrel of Europe, Asia, and Africa hunts house sparrows. Tawny owls do, too.

Common kestrel

BIRDS AS PESTS

S OME city-dwelling birds are not killers themselves, but may cause problems for humans anyway. Flocks of birds near airports may cause accidents to jets that are taking off. Airports have tried using machines, people, and peregrine falcons to keep birds away from the runways.

Flock of starlings

SCARE TACTICS

T HE mute swan is found in parks everywhere. It is 5 feet long, with snowy white feathers and a long, snakelike neck. This bird is very powerful and aggressive, especially when it is guarding its eggs or its young, called cygnets. It hisses and spits at intruders. A blow from its beating wings can break an arm.

Mute swan attacking duck

CROP-RAIDERS

SOME birds are thought of as killers because they destroy the crops people need to stay alive. Many birds rob farmers of fruit, peas and beans, and cereals such as wheat. Other birds, however, do humans a favor by killing insects that destroy crops.

THE SCOURGE OF AFRICA

CROP-RAIDING birds and insects can endanger human life in countries where there are already food shortages. In recent years, the countries south of the Sahara Desert in Africa have suffered from drought. Hungry animals have eaten away the plants, and the sands of the desert have drifted southward. Many people have died of starvation.

When crops are so important, the world's most destructive bird is not a welcome sight. The red-billed quelea is a sparrowlike bird with a big appetite. It eats grass seeds, millet, rice, and guinea corn. Queleas are also the world's most numerous birds. A single flock can number ten million. Many millions of queleas are killed every year, but that seems to have little effect on the problem.

Red-billed quelea

Quelea flock

SAVING THE BIRDS

B IRDS probably cause fewer problems for humans than do any other group of creatures. However, over the ages, some people have treated them as enemies.

Birds of prey kill out of necessity, not for pleasure. They depend on killing to stay alive. They never kill so much of one kind of prey that it becomes extinct.

Already many kinds of birds have disappeared from our planet forever. The American passenger pigeon was one of the most numerous birds in the world until the last century. Millions of them were shot. The last one died in 1914.

Many wild birds are still shot today, despite laws protecting some of them. Others, such as pheasant and grouse, are often bred simply to be shot for sport.

Even domestic birds that we raise for food and eggs are often kept in poor conditions.

Battery hens

Pheasants killed for sport

BIRDS AT RISK

ALTHOUGH some birds are bred in captivity, many others are still taken illegally from the wild to be used in falconry or kept as caged birds. Many states are passing laws to protect these birds. Egg collectors, too, have threatened the survival of many species of birds over the years. Nests of rare birds frequently must be guarded from poachers.

In recent years, the world of birds has increasingly been invaded by humans. We clear forests for farms or buildings. We destroy ancient forests for timber. We drain swamps, marshes, and other wetlands that are needed by predatory and migrating birds. We poison rivers and seas with waste and chemicals. We use insecticides and pesticides that may poison small mammals and birds. Birds of prey that feed on these smaller creatures may be poisoned themselves. We must make a greater effort to protect and preserve all kinds of birds.

Birds of prey facing extinction
★ Soumagne's owl
★ Monkey-eating eagle
★ Seychelles kestrel
★ Galapagos hawk
★ Californian condor (exist only in captivity)
★ Bald eagle

Fish, turtles, and dodos were collected for food.

INDEX

Africa 8, 9, 16, 18, 22, 23, 26, 28
aircraft 7, 27
Alaska 11
albatrosses 20
Andean condor 17
Antarctic 20
antelopes 7, 14, 16
Arctic 13, 15, 19, 20
Asia 13, 14, 16, 22, 24, 25, 26
Atlantic Ocean 21
attack 7, 20
Australia 9, 24

bald eagle 7, 11, 31
barn owl 18, 19
battery hens 30
beaks 7, 10, 11, 13, 18, 19, 20, 21, 22, 23, 24
birds of prey 6, 8, 10, 26, 30, 31
black-mantled goshawk 12
breeding 8, 15, 21
buzzards 13

Californian condor 17, 31
capybaras 15
caracaras 15
carrion 6, 7, 10, 11, 13, 15, 16, 17, 20, 24
cassowaries 9
Central America 15
chemicals 11, 19, 31
claws 7, 8, 9, 10, 16, 20
common buzzard 13
common cuckoo 25
common jay 24
common kestrel 26
condors 17
crested caracara 15

deer 7, 17
defense 7, 9, 20

eagle owl 18
eagles 6, 7, 10, 11, 14, 16
  true eagles 10
eared vulture 16
eggs 13, 20, 24, 25, 27
Egyptian vulture 16
Europe 13, 14, 16, 22, 24, 25, 26

falconry 14, 27, 31
falcons 14, 15, 16, 26, 27, 31
farmers 10, 19, 28
feathers 6, 10, 19, 27

fish 8, 10, 11, 18, 20, 21, 22
fish eagle 7, 10, 11, 20, 23
flightless birds 8, 9
forests 11, 12, 31
frigate bird 21
frogs 13, 22, 23
fulmar 20

gannet 21
giant kingfisher 23
golden eagle 10
goshawks 12
great blue heron 22
great frigate bird 21
great kingfisher 23
great skua 20
great white heron 22
Greenland 15
griffon vulture 16
grouse 15, 30
gull 20
gyrfalcon 15

harpy eagle 10, 11
harriers 13
hawks 13, 14, 25
  endangered 31
heron 22, 23
horned owl 18
hunting grounds 11

insecticides 11, 19, 31
insects 6, 18, 24, 25, 28, 31

kestrel 26
kingfishers 23

lambs 10, 15, 17
legs 8, 10, 12, 13, 15, 22, 23
lemmings 13, 19, 20
lizards 8, 13, 15, 22

man-o'-war birds 21
marsh harrier 13
martial eagle 7
Mauritius 30
mice 18, 19, 24
monkey-eating eagle 11
monkeys 11
Montagu's harrier 13
mountains 13
mute swan 27

nestlings 13, 19, 20, 21, 24, 25, 27
New Guinea 9, 12
Nile River 23

North Africa 13
Northern goshawk 12

ostriches 8
owls 18, 19
  true owls 18
  endangered 31

Pacific Ocean 11, 21
passenger pigeon 30
penguins 8, 20
peregrine falcon 14, 15, 27, 31
pheasants 30
Phillipine Islands 11
Pied currawong 24
pigeons 14, 26, 27

rabbits 10, 11, 13, 18
red-billed quelea 28
rodents 9, 10, 13, 15, 26
rough-necked buzzard 13

Sahara Desert 28
seabirds 20, 21
secretary bird 9
seeds 6, 8, 28
shoebill 23
skuas 20
snake-eating eagles 10
snakes 6, 9, 10, 13, 22
snowy owl 19
South America 15
sparrow hawk 12
sparrows 26, 28
spotted eagle owl 18
squirrels 11, 18
starlings 27
storks 22
  whale-headed stork 23
Sudan 23

talons 7, 12, 18, 19, 20
tawny owl 26
turtles 15, 21, 23

United States 11, 15, 16, 17, 22, 24, 30

vultures 16, 17
  New-World 16, 17
  Old-World 16

whale-headed stork 23
white-breasted sea eagle 6
white stork 22
wings 7, 9, 13, 14, 16, 17, 18, 27
woods 12, 13, 19, 24